United States Department of Agriculture

I0469862

Economic
Research
Service

Situation and
Outlook

LDP-M-256

Oct. 16, 2015

Livestock, Dairy, and Poultry Outlook

Kenneth Mathews
kmathews@ers.usda.gov

Mildred Haley
mhaley@ers.usda.gov

First Three Quarters of 2015 Show Red Meat and Poultry Production Higher

Contents

Tables

Web Sites

Animal Production and
Marketing Issues
Cattle
Dairy
Hogs
Poultry and Eggs
WASDE

Tables will be released
on Oct. 28, 2015

The next newsletter
release is Nov. 17, 2015

Approved by the
World Agricultural
Outlook Board.

As the last quarter of 2015 begins, production data show that total red meat and poultry production, aggregated over the first three quarters of 2015, increased by less than 1 percent over the same period of 2014. In the first three quarters of 2015, beef production is about 3 percent below production in the same period last year. Lower beef production is consistent with the early expansionary stage in the beef production cycle, during which females are retained for breeding rather than being slaughtered, thereby lowering beef production. Cattle prices so far in 2015 have averaged almost 3 percent above prices in the same period of 2014.

Production effects of disease outbreaks link the pork and poultry sectors, but in divergent directions: the pork sector continues to recover from the effects of porcine epidemic diarrhea (PEDv) outbreaks last year, with total production in the first three quarters of 2015 almost 8 percent ahead of the same period in 2014. The flip side of higher production is lower prices: 2015 hog prices have averaged more than 34 percent below prices of the first three quarters of 2014. The poultry sector is recovering from Highly Pathogenic Avian Influenza (HPAI), the effects of which has fallen so far on the turkey sector (2 percent lower production) and the egg sector (5 percent lower production). Turkey prices have averaged almost 6 percent above the same period last year; average egg prices are almost 36 percent above the same period of 2014. Broiler production is up in 2015 by 4 percent. Trade restrictions related to HPAI have generated large stocks, however, and domestic broiler prices have responded to the downside: whole bird composite prices are down more than 10 percent.

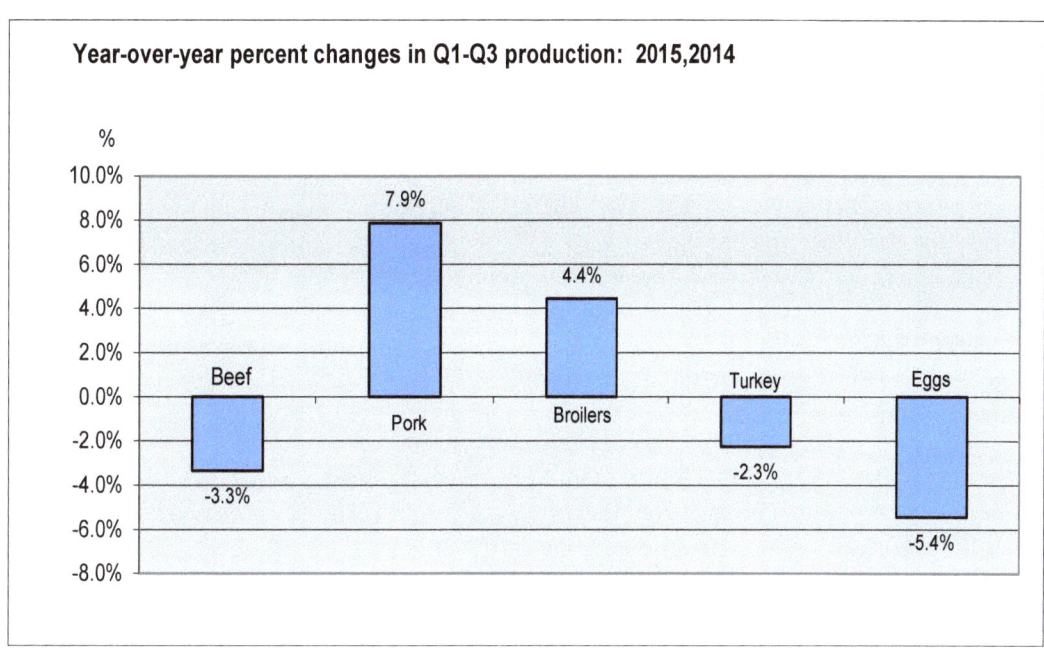

Year-over-year percent changes in Q1-Q3 production: 2015,2014

Source: USDA World Agricultural Supply and Demand Estimates. October 2015.

Beef/Cattle: Third-quarter 2015 fed cattle and feeder cattle prices declined sharply. Recent slaughter data indicates that cattle have been held back, allowing even further downward pressure on live cattle prices. Plunging prices have resulted in reductions in projected prices for 5-area direct, total all-grade steer prices to $129-$135/cwt.

Beef/Cattle Trade: U.S. beef exports continue to struggle, due primarily to a relatively strong dollar and decreased global demand for U.S. beef. However, exports are expected to have moderate growth in 2016 due to an expanding U.S. beef herd and slower growth in Australian beef exports to major trading partners. Strong beef imports for Australia and New Zealand continue to push U.S. beef imports higher. The January-August 2015 U.S. beef imports were approximately 32 percent higher than the same period last year.

Pork/Hogs: Subsequent to the release of the Quarterly Hogs and Pigs report on September 25, USDA raised 2016 pork production by 220 million pounds. The quarterly report detailed record-high inventories and litter rates. Pork exports in August were 6.5 percent greater than a year ago, based on strong shipments to Mexico and Asia.

Poultry: The combination of strong growth in U.S. broiler meat production and lower exports due to trade restrictions has continued to place downward pressure on broiler prices. August broiler meat production was up 7 percent from a year earlier to 3.4 billion pounds. U.S. turkey meat production in August 2015 was 451 million pounds, down 7 percent from a year earlier as turkey producers continue to deal with impacts of the Highly Pathogenic Avian Influenza (HPAI) outbreak earlier this year. Lower turkey meat production over the last several months has more than offset lower exports, lowering cold storage holdings. Table egg production in August was 545 million dozen, down 11 percent from a year earlier. The drop in production was due to decreases in both the size of the table egg flock (down 11 percent) and the average number of eggs per laying hen. Third-quarter egg prices averaged $2.36 per dozen, up 82 percent from the previous year.

Poultry Trade: Broiler, turkey, and egg shipments in August remained down from a year ago. Broiler shipments totaled 501 million pounds in August 2015, a decrease of 18 percent from a year earlier. Turkey shipments decreased 46 percent from a year ago, totaling 41 million pounds, while egg and egg product exports totaled 26 million dozen in August 2015, a 19-percent decrease from the previous August.

Sheep/Lamb: Choice slaughter lamb prices at San Angelo, Texas increased through the third quarter and are expected to show slight improvement through the fourth. Third-quarter 2015 commercial production of lamb and mutton is forecast at 37 million pounds, down nearly 3 percent from the same period in 2014. Imports of lamb and mutton remain strong, with the majority from Australia.

Dairy: The all-milk price forecast for the fourth quarter of 2015 is $17.00-$17.40 per cwt, an increase from $16.60-$17.10 forecast last month. The all-milk price for 2016 is $16.05-$16.95 per cwt, a reduction from $16.10-$17.10 forecast last month.

Recent Livestock, Dairy and Poultry Special Articles

"Effect of the Trans-Pacific Partnership on U.S. Dairy Trade," pdf pages 19-25 of November 2013 Livestock, Dairy and Poultry Outlook report (http://www.ers.usda.gov/media/1221780/specialarticleldpm233.pdf)

"Determinants of Japanese Demand for U.S. Pork Products in 2012," pdf pages 20-25 of the May 2013 Livestock, Dairy and Poultry Outlook report (http://www.ers.usda.gov/media/1106754/ldpm227.pdf)

Cattle Markets Collapse

Fed and feeder cattle market prices declined sharply late in the third quarter of 2015. For the week ending October 11, 2015, prices for 5-area all grades were $125.36/hundredweight (5-area Fed Steers, http://www.ams.usda.gov/mnreports/lm_ct150.txt), almost $40 lower than year-earlier fed steer prices. As with fed cattle, feeder cattle prices also took a hit. Oklahoma National Stockyards prices for medium number 1 feeder steers weighing 750-800 pounds ranged between $187-$192/cwt the week ending October 5, 2015, (http://www.ams.usda.gov/mnreports/ko_ls750.txt)—down more than $20 compared with the same time last year. Reasons for the sharp declines in fed cattle prices could include packer reluctance to pay higher prices during a time of softening beef prices and large supplies of heavyweight cattle. Mounting losses to cattle feeding are tempering demand for feeder cattle, pressuring feeder cattle prices downward. These plunging feeder calf prices will impact returns for cow-calf producers.

Pasture Conditions

Drought persists in much of the West and the Southern Plains, after a respite earlier in the year (Oct. 6, 2015 U.S. Drought Monitor). The October 6, 2015, U.S. Drought Monitor projected dry conditions to continue for the near term in Oklahoma and Eastern Texas. Through the week ending October 11, 2015, USDA Crop Progress reported that 23 percent of pasture and range conditions in the Lower 48 were rated as poor or very poor, slightly worse than the same time the previous year (http://usda.mannlib.cornell.edu/usda/current/CropProg/CropProg-10-13-2015.pdf). California, Oregon, and Washington each reported roughly 60 percent of their pasture and range conditions as poor or very poor. Ongoing drought could continue to adversely impact grazing in this region.

Despite abundant rainfall early in 2015, the recent lack of precipitation in the Southern Plains area may have an adverse impact on potential wheat pasture. For the first week of October, Oklahoma made the least progress in its winter wheat plantings but has caught up, according to the Crop Progress report for the week ending October 11, 2015. It was reported that 65 percent of winter wheat was planted in Oklahoma, down 12 percent compared with the same time last year and 1 percent below the 2010-2014 average. Texas reported 48 percent of its winter wheat planted, down 14 percent year over year and down 10 percent compared with the 4-year average. Many stocker operations depend on winter wheat grazing, but the current lack of rain has significantly delayed winter wheat emergence in the Southern Plains.

Placements and Marketings

The early portion of 2015 had favorable pasture conditions and good precipitation levels, allowing producers to graze cattle for longer than typical periods. Many of the cattle grazing in 2015 reached the feedlot at significantly higher weights. However, delayed winter wheat emergence could limit winter grazing availability for cattle located in the Southern Plains. This could reduce weights of feeder cattle placed in feedlots as absence of wheat pasture forces cattle into feedlots at younger ages and lighter weights. These lighter placements could also lead to lighter fed cattle and dressed weights being marketed in 2016.

Recent placements of feeder cattle in feedlots of 1,000-plus-head capacity in 2015 have been record lows for the series that began in 1996. August 2015 placements were 5 percent lower than August 2014, the lowest for August since the series began. Placements were low because producers kept cattle on pasture longer and generally to heavier weights, and feedlot operators have been resistant to paying high prices for feeders given their losses. The August 2015 category of 800-plus pounds for feeder cattle placements on feed were about 4 percent above August 2014. Because of relatively cheap corn prices, cattle feeders have had the opportunity to keep cattle on feed longer, which has resulted in increased cattle-on-feed inventories year over year.

Like August placements, August marketings of fed cattle were the lowest for August since the series began in 1996. Marketings of fed cattle during August totaled 1.59 million head, or 6 percent below 2014. Cattle feeders have little incentive to sell their animals at current price levels and may be holding on to fed cattle, hoping for better market prices.

Cattle in these increased cattle-on-feed inventories have also been marketed at atypically heavy weights, dampening cattle feeding margins. For example, the estimated breakeven price for October 2015 is $174.22/cwt (Cattle Feeder Simulator, http://www.ers.usda.gov/data-products/livestock-meat-domestic-data.aspx). With current prices, cattle feeders could lose as much as $50/cwt or more. Because of the recent collapse in fed cattle prices, USDA's third-quarter prices were reduced to $144.22/cwt—down $14 from this time last year. USDA revised fourth-quarter 2015 steer prices to $129-$135/cwt. Lower prices into early 2016 are expected to average $131-$141/cwt.

2015 5-Area Fed-Steer prices and 2015 Oklahoma City 750-800 pound Feeder-Steer prices
(Week ending 9/26/15)

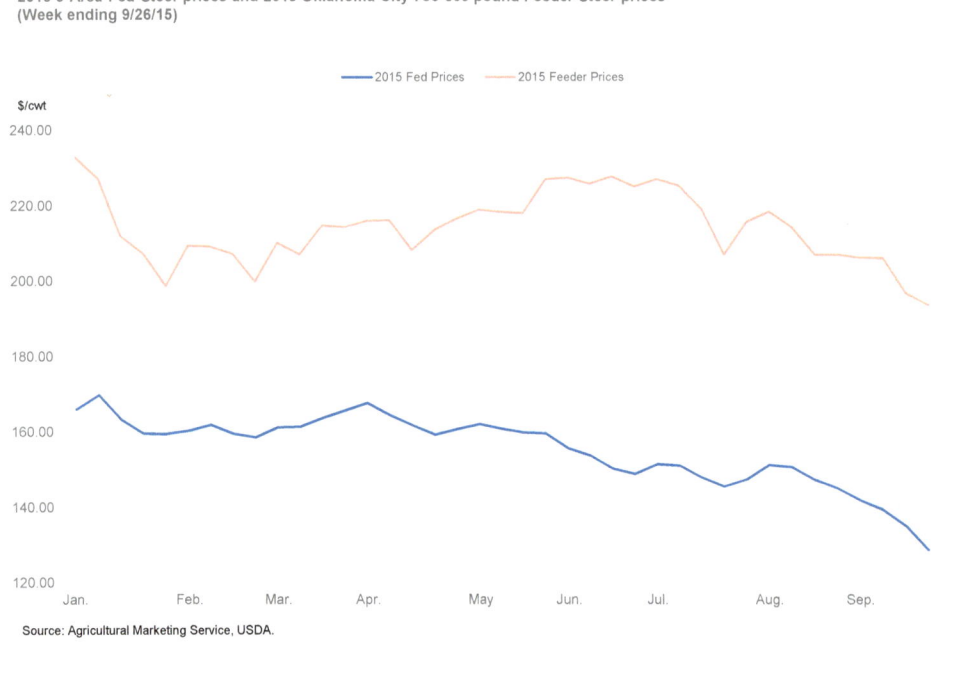

Source: Agricultural Marketing Service, USDA.

Weekly Beef Production Surpasses Year-Prior Levels

Cattle weights will continue to be an important factor to watch in the months ahead. Cattle are remaining on feed longer and are currently being marketed at record weights. This is being heightened by the increase in the proportion of heavier weight steers versus heifers and cows, resulting in near-term year-over-year increases in beef production despite the continuing constraint of cattle supplies. As of the week ending October 3rd, federally inspected cattle carcass weights were reported at 850 pounds, and weights are expected to remain at relatively high levels in the fourth quarter. In light of the factors mentioned above, the pace of marketings and heavy carcass weights, USDA revised third- and fourth-quarter beef production forecasts higher by 95 and 150 million pounds, respectively. USDA projects 2015 beef production will reach about 23.8 billion pounds. Higher cattle slaughter levels, in conjunction with heavy carcass weights, are expected to increase beef production in 2016. USDA's current forecast for total beef production next year is nearly 25.0 billion pounds, up 5 percent relative to 2015.

Wholesale Prices Plummet, Choice-Select Spread Narrows

The cattle and beef complex remains under immense pressure as a result of current supply and demand fundamentals. The abrupt decline in live cattle prices continues to support positive packer margins despite the simultaneous downturn in wholesale beef prices. The recent increase in year-over-year weekly beef production has been a drag on beef cutout values, but another factor helping to explain the decline in wholesale prices is weaker than expected beef demand. Beef primal values have declined sharply over the last month, some of which can be attributed to the seasonal transition from grilling items to roasting items. Record-heavy steer and heifer weights continue to pressure the 50-percent lean beef (50CL) market. The expected seasonal uptick in cow slaughter in the fourth quarter, brisk imports of lean processing beef, and large volumes of boneless beef in cold storage could result in further declines in the 90-percent lean beef (90CL) market. Choice and Select beef cutout values have declined steadily since late August, and the spread between the two has narrowed (approximately $5.51/cwt as of October 9th). Supportive of this squeeze is the current relationship between the percent of beef grading Choice or Select and the Choice-Select spread. The narrowing spread between the Choice-Select cutouts is logical due to the large amounts of Choice beef in the supply chain. Thus far in 2015, the percent of beef grading Choice has ranged between 68 and 70 percent and Select between 19 and 22 percent, whereas for the same period in 2014 Choice beef ranged between 64 and 68 percent and Select between 23 and 28 percent.

Weekly Federally Inspected Beef Production

Source: Agricultural Marketing Service, USDA.

Weekly Beef Cutout Values

Source: Agricultural Marketing Service, USDA.

Choice, Select Beef Grading, 2009-2015

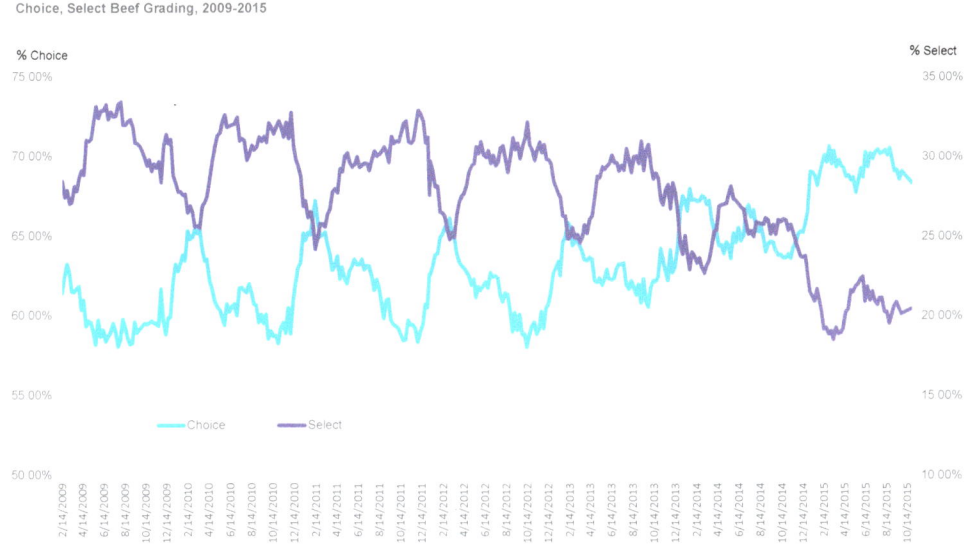

Source: Agricultural Marketing Service, USDA.

Limited Global Demand for U.S. Beef Constrains Exports; Beef Imports Remain Robust

Year-to-date U.S. beef exports through August are about 12 percent lower than the previous year. Lackluster demand from key trading partners continues to hamper U.S. beef exports. Exports to Japan, Hong Kong, and Mexico continue to experience strong declines year over year. Beef exports to Japan have declined approximately 12 percent (January-August 2015) from the previous year due to increased competition from Australian beef exports and the overall high price for U.S. beef. Exports to Mexico and Hong Kong are also lower by double-digit amounts. USDA revised third-quarter exports 25 million pounds lower on weaker than expected global demand from key trading partners, in part a function of the negative effect of the strong U.S. dollar and bearish global economic pressures. Total U.S. beef exports are forecast near 2.3 billion pounds in 2015, down 11 percent relative to 2014. However, exports are expected to improve in 2016 as U.S. beef supplies expand and domestic prices subside, spurring renewed global demand for U.S. beef. It is also expected that Australian beef exports will slow as producers begin to rebuild herds after an extended period of herd liquidation. Beef exports in 2016 are forecast at just over 2.4 billion pounds, up 6 percent over 2015.

U.S. beef imports for 2015 are forecast at 3.4 billion pounds, increasing nearly 17 percent year over year. Robust shipments of lean processing beef from Australia and New Zealand have propelled beef imports to historic levels. January-August 2015 beef imports from Australia and New Zealand are up 53 and 17 percent, respectively. In addition, beef imports from Canada, Mexico, Brazil and Uruguay are noticeably higher year to date. However, the brisk pace of U.S. beef imports is expected to slow substantially in 2016 as a result of sharp reductions in processing beef imports from Australia. Australia has experienced massive herd liquidation due to extreme drought conditions that began in 2012, and, as a result, is faced with shrinking beef cattle inventories. Smaller cattle inventory levels will translate into decreased slaughter and beef production next year, with subsequent lower exports for Australia. In addition, expanding domestic U.S. beef supplies are expected to limit beef import demand in 2016. Beef imports for 2016 are projected to reach 3.0 billion pounds, down 11 percent relative to 2015.

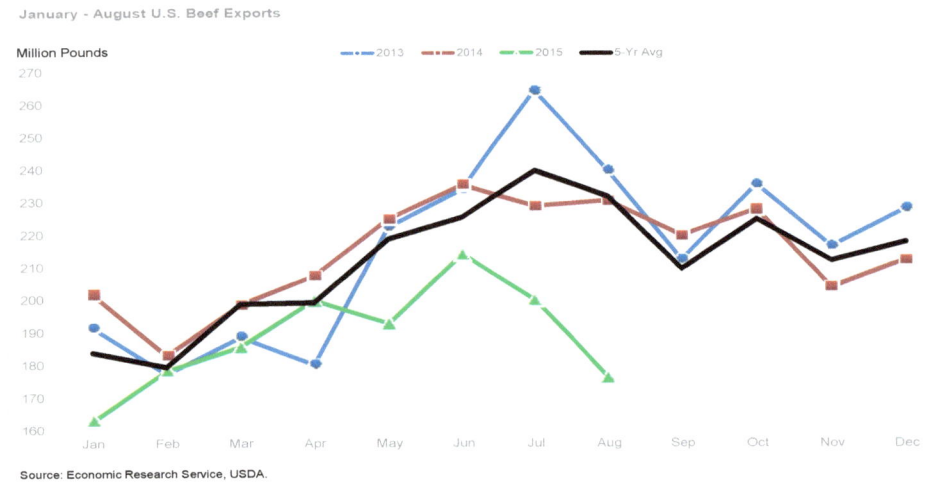

January - August U.S. Beef Exports

Source: Economic Research Service, USDA.

January - August U.S. Beef Imports

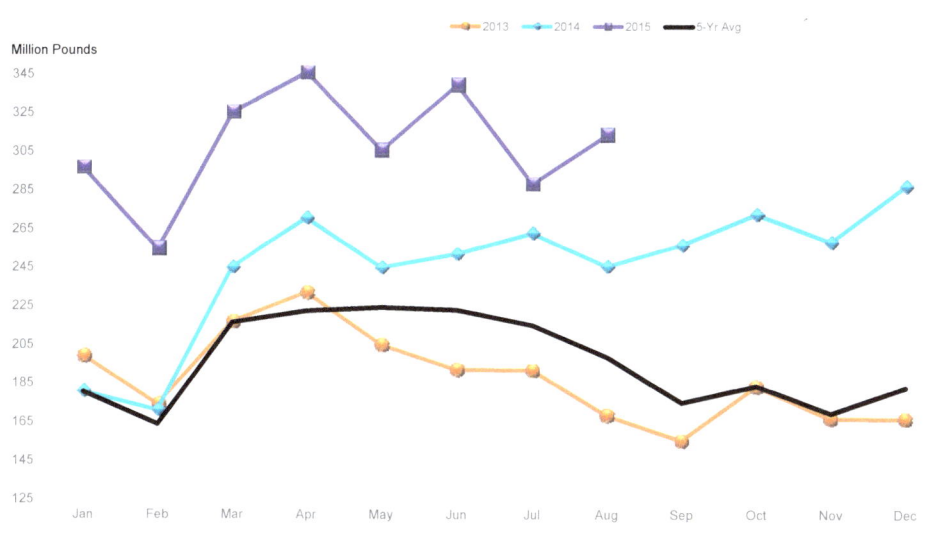

Source: Economic Research Service, USDA.

September Quarterly Hogs and Pigs Shows Record Inventories and Litter Rates

The *Quarterly Hogs and Pigs* report published by USDA on September 25 provided further evidence that the U.S. pork industry has largely moved beyond the disease problems that hampered production in 2014. The report showed record-high inventories of hogs and pigs (4 percent above numbers a year ago) and continued expansion in the breeding inventory (1 percent higher than a year ago), along with record-high litter rates. An important consequence of the September report is that USDA raised its forecast for 2016 pork production by about 220 million pounds to 25 billion pounds, an increase of 1.4 percent over production this year.

The September report indicates that the production increases this year, and those expected in 2016, are the product of both industry expansion (i.e., more sows) and increasing litter rates. In 2013—the year before significant effects of Porcine Epidemic Diarrhea (PEDv) were apparent—the number of breeding animals averaged 5.84 million head. The average number of breeding animals estimated for the current year (December 1, 2014, March 1, 2015, June 1, 2015 and September 1, 2015), was about 5.96 million head, an increase of about 120,000 animals or 2 percent. The inventory of breeding animals on September 1, 2015 was the largest since 2008.

The figure below shows that litter rates have more than recovered from the effects of PEDv. The pigs per litter rate for the June-August quarter, at 10.39, was record-high, having broken the record set in the preceding March-May quarter. For perspective, however, USDA's most recent *United States and Canadian Hogs* report http://usda.mannlib.cornell.edu/usda/current/USCH/USCH-08-20-2015.pdf, released August 20, 2015, implied that 2015 Canadian litter rates averaged 10.9 pigs per litter. On the other hand, anecdotal evidence abounds that many Corn Belt farrowing operations now routinely exceed U.S. national averages. U.S. litter rates are expected to continue to increase and to be a source of 2016 pork production growth.

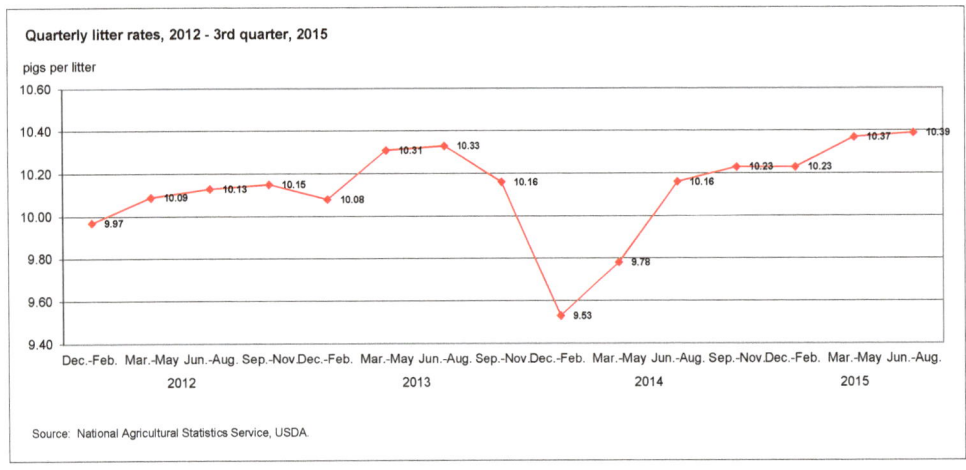

Quarterly litter rates, 2012 - 3rd quarter, 2015

Source: National Agricultural Statistics Service, USDA.

August Pork Exports Solid with Strong Shipments to Mexico and Asia

U.S. pork exports in August were 373 million pounds, 6.5 percent greater than a year ago. Shipments to Mexico (+15 percent), Japan (+4 percent) China-Hong Kong (+22 percent), and South Korea (+12 percent) were key in pushing exports above year-earlier levels for the fourth time this year.

Although August exports to China-Hong Kong—at 29 million pounds—were larger than a year ago, shipments so far in 2015 have been lackluster. Total U.S. pork exports to China-Hong Kong in the first 8 months of 2015 were more than 35 percent lower than in the same period last year. China import data from the Global Trade Atlas (GTA) shows that Chinese pork imports, through August are almost 16 percent higher than a year ago. So who is capturing market share from U.S. pork? The GTA data show that in the first 8 months of 2014 the European Union accounted for 62 percent of Chinese imports, while the United States held a 24-percent share. However, over the same period of 2015, the EU accounted for a 73-percent share of China's import market—a gain of roughly 11 percentage points—compared with the United States' 2015 share of 17 percent, a loss of about 7 percentage points. Canada also appears to have ceded market share this year to the E.U. (Due to rounding, market shares do not total to exactly 100.)

Importers base buying decisions on many factors, but price is often chief among them. Recent relative exchange-rate changes between the U.S. dollar and the Euro likely make European pork products cheaper to Chinese buyers. Further, China's delisting of numerous U.S. plants and zero tolerance for Ractopamine residues continue to limit opportunities for U.S. pork.

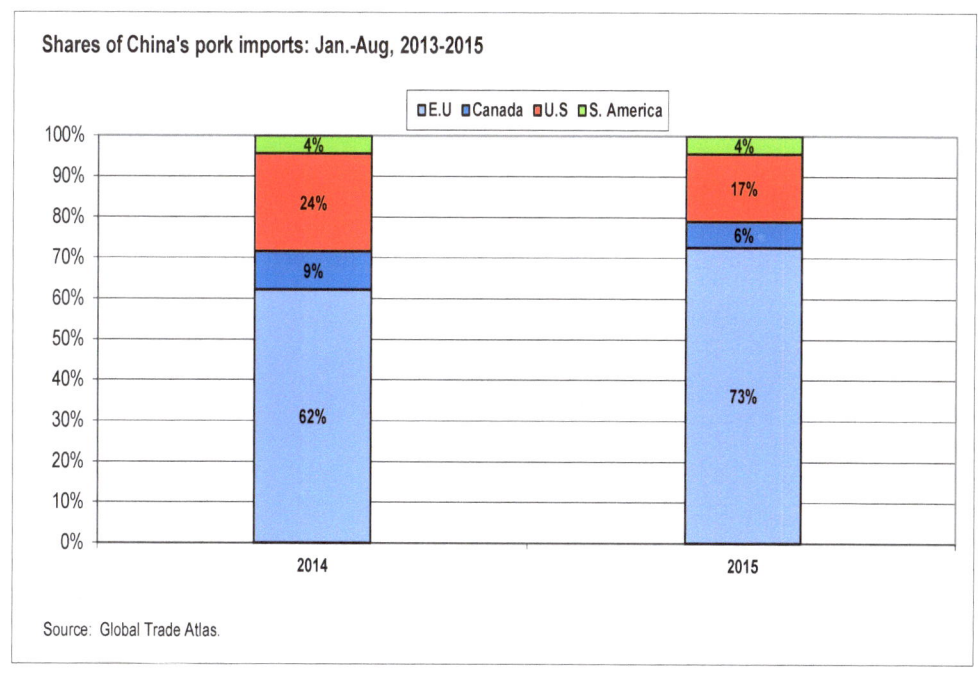

Shares of China's pork imports: Jan.-Aug, 2013-2015

Source: Global Trade Atlas.

Exchange rate: Euro\U.S. dollar

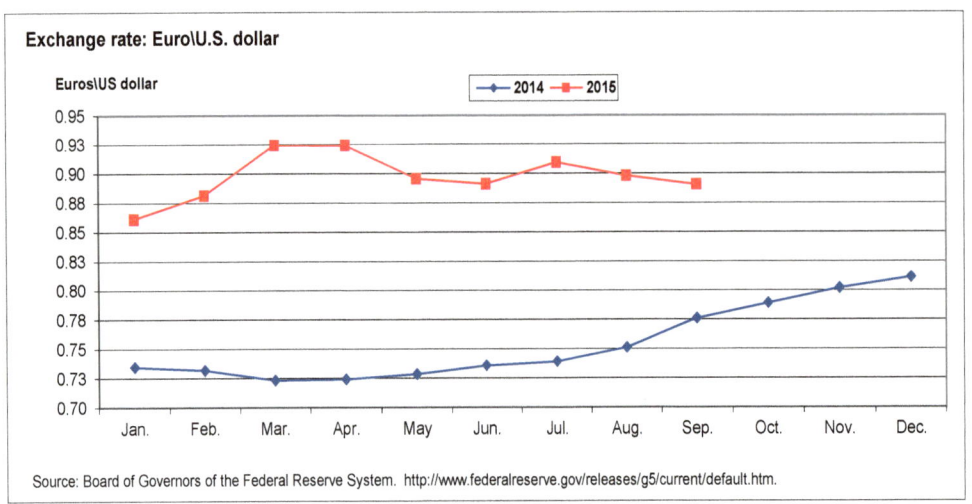

Source: Board of Governors of the Federal Reserve System. http://www.federalreserve.gov/releases/g5/current/default.htm.

Broiler Meat Production Climbs in August

U.S. broiler meat production in August totaled 3.4 billion pounds, 7 percent higher than the previous year. The increase was largely attributed to a higher number of birds slaughtered. In August, the number of birds slaughtered was 741 million, up 4 percent from the previous year. The size of the increase was unexpected as data from the NASS Broiler Hatchery report had seemed to point to a smaller gain. In addition to the increase in number, average live bird weights at slaughter continued higher than the previous year. In August, it was 6.12 pounds, a gain of 2 percent from a year earlier

With the higher than expected broiler meat production in August, the estimate for production in third-quarter 2015 was increased by 50 million pounds to 10.275 billion pounds. However, slower increases in the number of birds going to slaughter are expected in fourth-quarter 2015 and the first half of 2016. The production forecast for fourth-quarter 2015 was reduced by 25 million pounds to 10.025 billion pounds, and the production forecast for the first half of 2016 was lowered by 100 million pounds. The forecast for the second half of 2016 was also reduced by 75 million pounds.

The most recent 5-week average for the number of broiler chicks being placed for growout (September 5 to October 3) is only fractionally lower (0.2 percent) than the same period a year earlier; over the last several weeks, the number of eggs placed in incubators has been at or below the level of the previous year. While the number of birds going to slaughter later this year is expected to be close to that of a year earlier, average weights are expected to remain higher than the previous year.

At the end of August, cold storage holdings of broiler meat products totaled 738 million pounds, 24 percent higher than a year earlier. With geater production and lower exports, stock levels have been significantly higher for most of the year. The higher cold storage holdings at the end of August stemmed from larger stocks in each of the categories reported, with only drumsticks and wings having increases of less than 10 percent. The largest factors in the increase, in terms of poundage, were 21-percent larger holdings of breast meat, a 17-percent gain in leg quarter holdings and a year-over-year gain of 31 percent in holdings in the "other" categories. Cold storage holding are expected to increase, with fourth-quarter 2015 ending stocks forecast at 765 million pounds as the year-over-year growth in production slows and exports begin to gradually increase.

Higher production and lower exports have resulted in growing stock levels, which in turn have placed downward price pressure on wholesale prices. Prices for almost all broiler products are down significantly from the previous year. Prices for whole broilers averaged $0.77 per pound in September, down almost $0.30 per pound (28 percent) and leg quarter prices fell to less than $0.25 per pound in the Northeast market, 46 percent lower than the previous year. Only wing prices were higher than the previous year, but they were only fractionally more in September after being significantly higher over the first 8 months of 2015.

Wholesale broiler prices are forecast to remain under downward price pressure until lower growth in production and gradually increasing exports combine to reduce supplies of broiler products in cold storage. In third-quarter 2015, the price of whole broilers declined to $0.84 per pound, about $0.21 per pound lower (20 percent) than a year earlier. Whole bird prices are forecast to fall to $0.73-$0.77 per pound in fourth-quarter 2015 and remain below the previous year for the first half of 2016, but then to move higher in the second half of the year.

Turkey Meat Production Falls in August

U.S. turkey meat production in August 2015 was 451 million pounds, down 7 percent from a year earlier as turkey producers continued to deal with the impacts of the HPAI outbreak earlier this year. The decrease in production was due to a combination of a lower number of birds slaughtered and a drop in the average live weight per bird at slaughter. In August 19.3 million turkeys were slaughtered, down 4 percent from a year earlier, the fourth consecutive month in which the number of birds slaughtered was below the previous year. The August average live weight at slaughter was lower at 29.2 pounds, down 3 percent from the previous year, the fifth consecutive month with average weights lower than the year before. With the slightly lower than expected turkey meat production in August, the forecast for third-quarter 2015 was reduced by 25 million pounds to 1.325 billion, 10 percent lower than the previous year.

Turkey production is projected to decline again on a year-over-year basis in fourth-quarter 2015 and in first-quarter 2016. Overall production in 2016 is forecast at 6.01 billion pounds, 8 percent higher than in 2015. The growth in production will be mostly in the second half of the year. With relatively low feed costs and generally strong prices for whole birds and parts, the forecast is for turkey producers to have an incentive to increase production through most of 2016.

At the end of August, cold storage holdings of turkey products totaled 476 million pounds, 4 percent lower than at the same time in 2014. With a strong decline in production forecast for third-quarter 2015, turkey holdings are forecast to be lower than the previous year in fourth-quarter 2015 and in first-quarter 2016. On a year-over-year basis, turkey cold storage holdings have been lower than the previous year for 2 of the last 3 months as lower production has more than offset declines in turkey exports. While turkey cold storage holdings were lower than the previous year, stocks were also down 18 million pounds from the previous month. At this point in the year, turkey cold storage holdings are beginning to move out of public cold storage into private cold storage holdings as retailers begin to prepare for the Thanksgiving holiday. While the holdings were not all whole turkeys, they accounted for 7 million pounds of the decline. At the end of August, cold storage holdings of whole birds totaled 289 million pounds, 4 percent lower than a year earlier. The decline in whole bird stocks from the end of July to the end of August came entirely from a decline in stocks of whole hens, as stocks of whole toms rose slightly. On a year-over-year basis, stocks of whole hens were 160 million pounds at the end of August, 3 percent lower than a year earlier, while cold storage holdings of whole toms were 129 million pounds, 6 percent lower than a year earlier. Although the annual seasonal reduction in cold storage holdings seems to have begun somewhat earlier than in past years, the forecast for ending stocks for fourth-quarter 2015 remains at 190 million pounds, down slightly from the previous year.

Lower production over the last several months has offset lower turkey exports and translated into slightly lower stock levels. The lower stocks have resulted in upward pressure on prices for whole birds and some parts. The average price for frozen whole hen turkeys (National price 8-16 lbs.) was $1.26 per pound in third-quarter 2015, 16 cents more per pound than a year earlier (up 15 percent). The wholesale price in fourth-quarter 2015 is forecast at $1.31-$1.37 per pound, about 20 cents higher than the previous year.

Lower cold storage holdings have also placed upward price pressure on some turkey parts. In August, prices for boneless/skinless turkey breasts were 40 percent higher than a year earlier and averaged about $5.60 per pound. Prices for bone-in breasts were also higher, but the price of drumsticks had fallen significantly from the previous year, with frozen tom drumsticks averaging $0.66 per pound, down 26 percent. With overall turkey stocks forecast lower than the previous year through the end of 2015, many turkey parts will continue to have upward price pressure until production begins rising in 2016.

Table Egg Production Down, Hatching Egg Production Higher

In August, U.S. table egg production was 545 million dozen, down 11 percent from a year earlier. The drop in production was due to decreases in both the size of the table egg flock (down 11 percent) and the number of eggs per hen (down less than 1 percent). In August, the number of hens in the table egg laying flock was 272 million, well below the previous year but up slightly from the previous month as egg producers gradually begin to rebuild table egg flocks. Table egg production was higher during first-quarter 2015, but it then fell due to the HPAI outbreak and has been down between 11 and 12 percent during the last 3 months. Table egg production is forecast to be lower than the previous year through the remainder of 2015 and during first-quarter 2016; it is then forecast to start increasing in the remaining three quarters of 2016.

Over the first 8 months of 2015, hatching egg production totaled 740 million dozen, 4 percent higher than the same period in 2014. The gain has been relatively evenly divided between increases in broiler-type eggs (up 4 percent) and egg-type eggs (up 5 percent). Production of hatching eggs is forecast to total 285 million dozen in third-quarter 2015. This is a slight increase (5 million dozen) from the earlier forecast and up about 13 million dozen from the previous year. Hatching egg production is forecast higher than the previous year through the first half of 2016 chiefly due to increases in broiler-type hatching eggs and strong increases in egg-type egg production. Overall hatching egg production in the second half of 2016 is forecast be to about the same as in second half 2015.

In September, wholesale prices for a dozen large eggs in the New York market averaged $2.23, leaving average prices in third-quarter 2015 at $2.36 per dozen, up 81 percent from a year earlier. By early October, prices had moved considerably lower than their September average, falling to around $1.56 per dozen. The forecast for fourth-quarter 2015 was lowered from the previous forecast and is expected to average $2.22-$2.32 per dozen, still up 40 percent from the previous year as prices are expected to rise during the Thanksgiving-Christmas holiday period. Egg prices are forecast to average well above the previous year through the first half of 2016, but then to be considerably lower in the second half as flocks are rebuilt and production increases.

U.S. Broiler Shipments Down in August

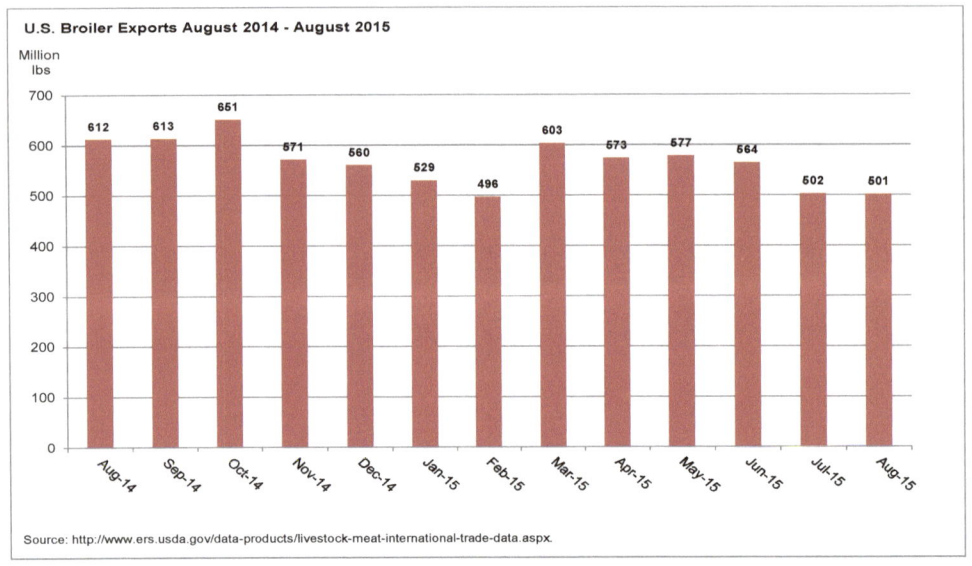

U.S. Broiler Exports August 2014 - August 2015

Million lbs

Aug-14	612
Sep-14	613
Oct-14	651
Nov-14	571
Dec-14	560
Jan-15	529
Feb-15	496
Mar-15	603
Apr-15	573
May-15	577
Jun-15	564
Jul-15	502
Aug-15	501

Source: http://www.ers.usda.gov/data-products/livestock-meat-international-trade-data.aspx

Broiler shipments dropped 18 percent in August compared with a year earlier, totaling 501 million pounds. Exports to Mexico, the United States' largest market, declined by 1 percent from August 2014 levels at 122 million pounds. National bans by China, Russia, and South Korea continue to impact exports. August trade also included the temporary loss of U.S. exports to Cuba, which reportedly suspended imports from the United States between August and September. Cuba had averaged 24 million pounds of monthly broiler shipments from the United States in 2015 through July. Most major markets were down or flat from a year earlier, but increased exports to Taiwan (+59% compared with August 2014), Guatemala (+36%), Iraq (+113%), Haiti (+37%), and Kazakhstan (+61%) provided some relief. The forecast for 2015 broiler exports was reduced 125 million pounds to 6.59 billion pounds as the pace of trade recovery has been slower than expected, while the forecast for 2016 was reduced 50 million pounds to 7.10 billion pounds.

Turkey Exports Drop in August from a Year Earlier

In August, turkey exports totaled 41 million pounds, 46 percent lower than the previous August. The decrease was mainly due to a sharp decline in exports to Mexico, the largest market for U.S. turkey products. The 29 million pounds shipped to Mexico in August were 37 percent lower than the previous August. The overall decline in exports in August was likely due to the decline in production caused by HPAI outbreaks in spring 2015 and bans on imports from U.S. States where there have been outbreaks. The forecast for 2015 turkey exports was reduced by 5 million pounds to 537 million pounds, while the 2016 forecast is unchanged at 740 million pounds. Exports in 2016 are expected to recover modestly as producers regain production capacity following the 2015 HPAI outbreak.

Egg Exports Down in August

Total egg exports (shell eggs and egg products) reached the shell egg equivalent of 26 million dozen in August, 19 percent lower than the previous year. The decline was primarily due to a sharp decrease in exports to Mexico, Japan, and Hong Kong. Shipments to Mexico were 52 percent lower in August compared with a year earlier, while shipments to Japan and Hong Kong fell by 65 percent and 63 percent, respectively. In contrast, shipments to Canada increased by 78 percent compared with a year earlier, totaling 15 million dozen. Egg exports in 2015 are now expected to total 322 million dozen as decreased production, high domestic prices, and trade bans are expected to continue to limit exports. The forecast for 2016 exports remains at 350 million dozen.

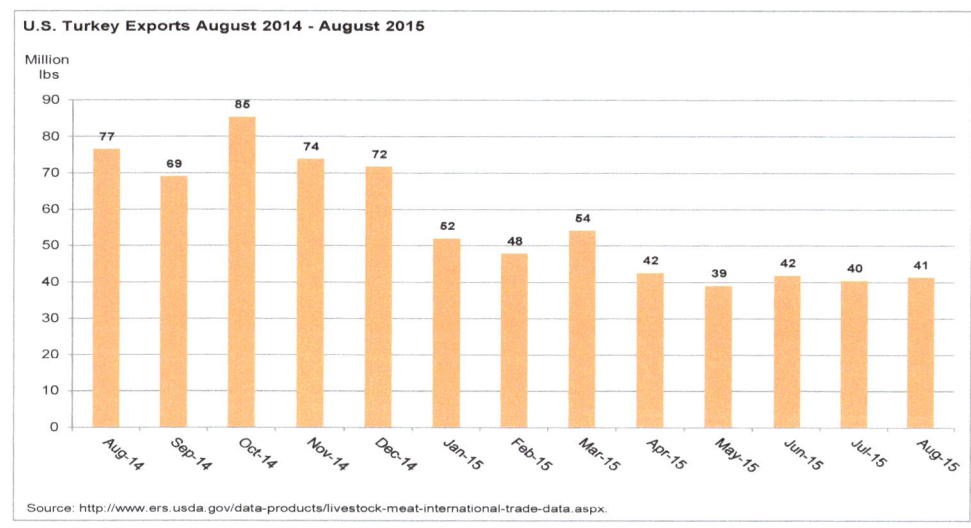

U.S. Turkey Exports August 2014 - August 2015

Source: http://www.ers.usda.gov/data-products/livestock-meat-international-trade-data.aspx.

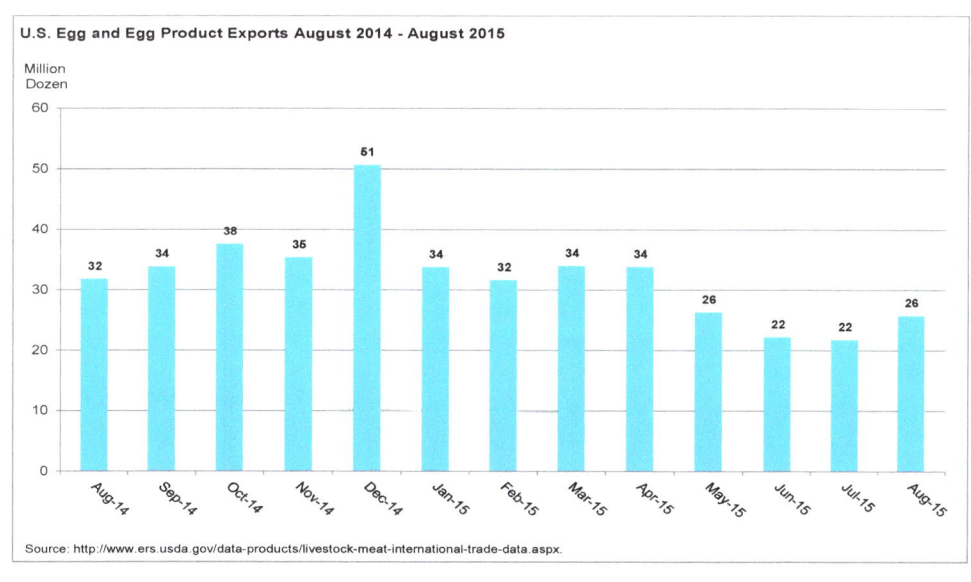

U.S. Egg and Egg Product Exports August 2014 - August 2015

Source: http://www.ers.usda.gov/data-products/livestock-meat-international-trade-data.aspx.

2015 Slaughter Lamb Prices Below 2014 Levels

Slaughter Lamb Price

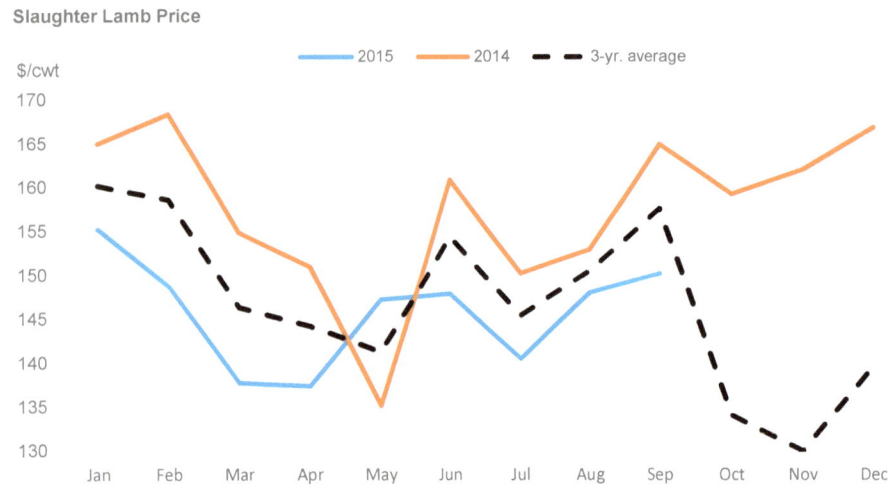

Source: Agricultural Marketing Service, USDA.

Unlike in 2014, most slaughter lamb market prices thus far in 2015 have been below the 3-year average. Third-quarter 2015 Choice slaughter lamb prices at San Angelo, Texas have ranged between $140-150/cwt despite tighter supplies, strengthening in each month of the quarter. The increasing strength in slaughter lamb prices is likely due to greater demand and an infusion of younger market-ready higher quality lambs. In July, the slaughter lamb price was $140.50/cwt and in August it was $147.88/cwt. The third-quarter 2015 slaughter lamb price averaged $146.23/cwt. A seasonal upswing in slaughter lamb prices is expected for the fourth quarter due to the customary increase in lamb demand in the year-end holiday period. Fourth-quarter 2015 slaughter lambs are forecast between $149-$155/cwt.

Slight Reduction in Lamb and Mutton Production

Third-quarter 2015 commercial lamb and mutton production is forecast at 37 million pounds, down nearly 3 percent from the same period in 2014. Commercial production was 12.9 million pounds in July 2015 and 11.7 million pounds in August. It was estimated that September 2015 commercial production would be around 12 million pounds. There is a marked decline in the number of animals slaughtered in federally inspected plants during third quarter 2015 relative to last year. In July, 166,800 head of sheep were slaughtered –down almost 12 percent from the same period in 2014—while in August 155,000 head were slaughtered–roughly 4-percent fewer than in the same period in 2014. Preliminary data suggest that slaughter in September will be down relative to last year.

2015 Lamb and Mutton Trade

Imports of lamb and mutton remain strong despite record stocks in cold storage. Based on the NASS Cold Storage report, September, 2015 beginning stocks for lamb and mutton were 41.9 million pounds, roughly 4 percent higher year over year. Australia and New Zealand remain the major suppliers of imported lamb and mutton. Second-quarter 2015 saw a spike in imports of roughly 56 million pounds, perhaps due to the strong U.S. dollar and weaker sales to China. In addition, Australia and New Zealand are experiencing drought conditions and are liquidating at a higher than normal rate. Third-quarter 2015 imports are forecast to decline to 43 million pounds, about 4 percent below a year earlier. This is due to the expectation of a declining rate of liquidation in Australia.

Lamb and mutton exports for the second quarter were 1 million pounds, and third quarter exports are also forecast at 1 million pounds, down 50 percent compared with third quarter exports in 2014. Fourth-quarter exports are expected to be about double the 2014 levels, due to increased holiday season demand from Mexico and the Caribbean Islands.

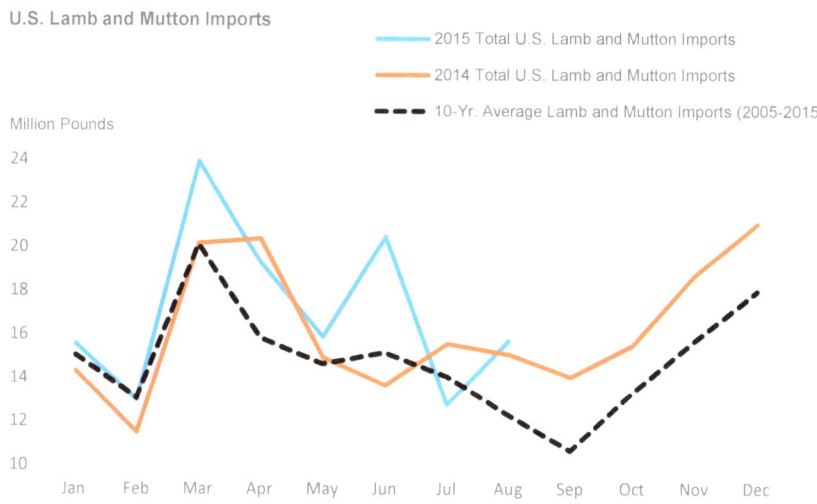

U.S. Lamb and Mutton Imports

2015 Total U.S. Lamb and Mutton Imports
2014 Total U.S. Lamb and Mutton Imports
10-Yr. Average Lamb and Mutton Imports (2005-2015)

Source: Agricultural Marketing Service, USDA.

Recent Developments in Dairy Markets

Average national wholesale prices for basic dairy products, as reported by USDA Agricultural Marketing Service (AMS), moved in mixed directions from August to September. The cheddar cheese price decreased from $1.739 to $1.715 per pound. The nonfat dry milk (NDM) price rose from the low level of $0.744 to $0.801 per pound. The dry whey price fell substantially from $0.311 to $0.244 per pound. The greatest change was in the butter price, which rose from $2.044 to $2.445 per pound.

Notably, the daily Chicago Mercantile Exchange (CME) spot price for butter spiked over a few days to a record high of $3.135 per pound on September 25, but the price fell substantially thereafter. The AMS September national average butter price of $2.445 per pound was much higher than average export prices, as reported by AMS Dairy Market News: $1.357 per pound for Oceania and $1.309 per pound for Europe.

With large price differences between the domestic price and foreign export prices, butter imports have grown to high levels, even at the high-tier tariff rate of about $0.70 per pound[1]. For January through August 2015, licensed imports were 11.8 million pounds, high-tier butter imports were 12.4 million pounds, and imports under free trade agreements were 2.1 million pounds. With butter imports exceeding a trigger level of about 20.8 million pounds, a safeguard duty of $0.233 per pound has been implemented, effective from October 5 through December 31, 2015 (http://www.gpo.gov/fdsys/pkg/FR-2015-10-05/html/2015-25235.htm).[2]

Wholesale prices for butter

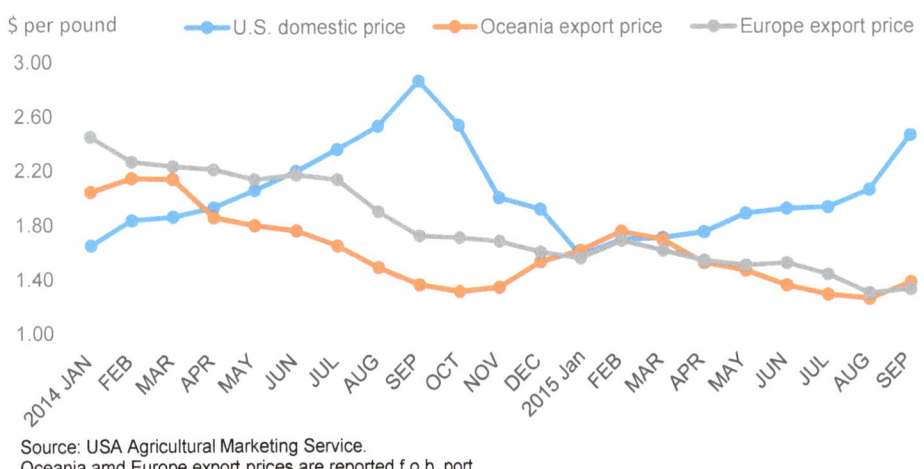

Source: USA Agricultural Marketing Service.
Oceania amd Europe export prices are reported f.o.b. port.

---

[1] Most dairy products are subject to tariff rate quotas (TRQs), which allow imports at a relatively low tariff level within a set quota. Imports outside of the quota are charged a high-tier tariff rate. A license is required for most in-quota dairy imports. Importers importing without a license pay the higher rate.

[2] If the goods have a contract for carriage dated prior to midnight October 4, 2015, they are exempt from quantitative safeguard quota.

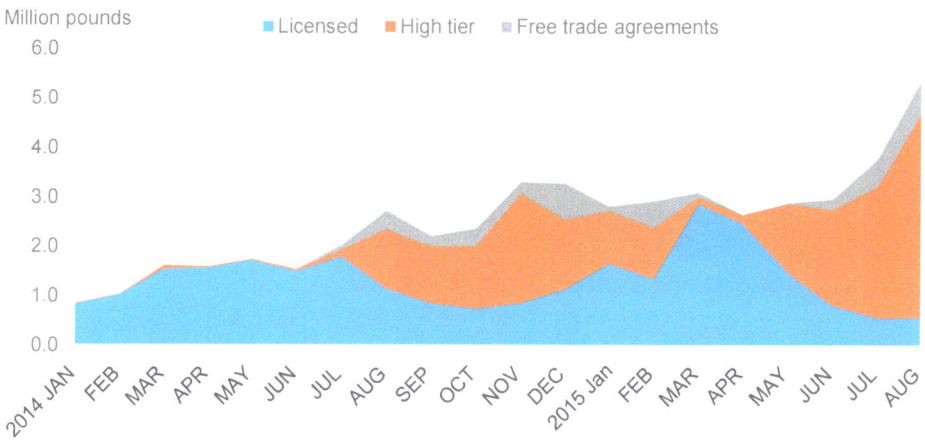

U.S. butter imports

Million pounds

Legend: Licensed | High tier | Free trade agreements

Sources: U.S Census Bureau data as reported by USDA Foreign Agricultural Service and U.S. International Trade Commission.

Milk production for August was 0.8 percent above August 2014. While year-over-year milk production increased for most States, it was notably lower in California (-3.4 percent) and New Mexico (-4.3 percent). Notably, August ending stocks for cheese and dry whey were higher than August 2014 levels by 12 percent and 43 percent, respectively.

Feed Price Situation for Dairy

The 2015/16 forecast for corn is raised from last month to $3.50-$4.10 per bushel. The soybean meal price forecast is unchanged at $310-$350 per short ton. The alfalfa hay price fell from $169 to $159 per short ton from July to August.

Dairy Forecasts for the Remainder of 2015

Recent milk production data are consistent with last month's expectations. The 2015 milk production forecasts for the remainder of the year are unchanged from last month. For the fourth quarter, milk production is forecast at 51.6 billion pounds, with cow numbers at 9.325 million head and a yield of 5,530 pounds per cow.

With domestic demand expected to support higher imports of butter and cheese, the expectation for imports on a milk-fat milk-equivalent basis for the third quarter has been raised by 0.1 billion pounds, while the projection is unchanged for the fourth quarter. The expectation for third-quarter imports on a skim-solids milk-equivalent basis has been lowered by 0.1 billion pounds, and the fourth quarter forecast has been lowered by 0.1 billion pounds based on lower expected imports of milk protein concentrate.

On a milk-fat basis, expectations for exports have been lowered by 0.2 billion pounds for the third quarter based on weaker cheese sales, and the projection is unchanged for the fourth quarter. On a skim-solids basis, expectations for exports have been lowered by 0.2 billion pounds for the third quarter based upon lower expected cheese and whey exports, and the forecast is unchanged for the fourth quarter.

Ending stock forecasts for 2015 have been raised by 0.1 billion pounds on a milk-fat basis and 0.2 billion pounds on a skim-solids basis. Changes in stock levels are based upon high ending cheese stocks for August and lower expected exports.

Fourth-quarter price forecasts for cheese and NDM have been raised to $1.705-$1.745 and $0.900-$0.940 per pound, respectively. Although the third-quarter butter price was higher than expected, the fourth-quarter forecast has been lowered to $2.080-$2.150 per pound as declines are expected to continue in the near term. The whey price forecast for the fourth quarter has been lowered significantly to 21.5-23.5 cents per pound based upon recent price data and high stock levels.

With the higher cheese price forecast more than offsetting the lower whey price, the Class III milk price forecast for the fourth quarter has been raised to $15.45-$15.85 per cwt. With the higher forecast NDM price more than offsetting the lower butter price, the Class IV milk price has been raised to $14.45-$14.95 per cwt. The all-milk price forecast for the fourth quarter is $17.00-$17.40 per cwt, an increase from $16.60-$17.10 forecast last month.

Dairy Forecasts for 2016

Changes from last month's 2016 forecasts for supply and use are relatively small. The milk production forecast for 2016 is unchanged at 213.0 billion pounds, a 1.8 percent year-over-year increase, adjusted for leap year. Milk cows are expected to average 9.310 million head, with a yield per cow of 22,880 pounds. Global competition is expected to remain strong in 2016. Export forecasts for 2016 are unchanged from last month. Forecasts for imports are raised by 0.2 billion pounds on a milk-fat basis and lowered by 0.1 billion pounds on a skim-solids basis. Domestic commercial use forecasts have been raised by 0.2 billion pounds on both a milk-fat and skim-solids basis.

The 2016 forecasts for butter, cheese, and NDM are higher than last month at $1.840-$1.960, $1.600-$1.690, and $0.960-$1.030 per pound, respectively. The forecast for dry whey has been lowered to 28.0-31.0 cents per pound. The Class III milk price forecast has been lowered to $14.75-$15.65 per cwt, as the decrease in the dry whey price forecast more than offsets the higher price forecasts of the other contributing dairy products. With higher price forecasts for butter and NDM, the Class IV milk price forecast has been raised to $13.95-14.95 per cwt. With a lower Class III price more than offsetting the higher Class IV price, the all-milk price forecast has been lowered to $16.05-$16.95 per cwt, a decrease from $16.10-$17.10 forecast last month.

Trans-Pacific Partnership

On October 7, 2015, the U.S. and 11 Pacific Rim nations concluded negotiations for the Trans-Pacific Partnership. Member countries include the United States, Australia, Brunei Darussalam, Canada, Chile, Japan, Malaysia, Mexico, New Zealand, Peru, Singapore, and Vietnam. The agreement would eliminate or significantly reduce tariffs on globally traded products and deter non-science based sanitary and phytosanitary trade barriers. The agreement is subject to ratification by the member countries. For more information, see http://www.fas.sda.gov/tpp.

USDA Extends Dairy Margin Protection Program Deadline

On September 22, 2015, Agriculture Secretary Tom Vilsack announced that the deadline to enroll for the Dairy Margin Protection Program for coverage in 2016 has been extended until Nov. 20, 2015. The voluntary program, established by the 2014 Farm Bill, provides financial assistance to participating farmers when the margin—the difference between the price of milk and feed costs—falls below the coverage level selected by the farmer. To enroll in the program, a dairy farmer needs to contact a local USDA Service Center. A locator is available at http://offices.sc.egov.usda.gov/locator/app.

Contact Information

Ken Mathews (coordinator, cattle/beef and veal)	(202) 694-5183	kmathews@ers.usda.gov
Sahar Angadjivand (beef/cattle and veal)	(202) 694-5187	sangadjivand@ers.usda.gov
Seanicaa Edwards (beef/cattle and beef/cattle trade)	(202) 694-5333	seanicaa.edwards@ers.usda.gov
Alex Melton (poultry trade)	(202) 694-5409	awmelton@ers.usda.gov
Mildred M. Haley (coordinator, hogs/pork)	(202) 694-5176	mhaley@ers.usda.gov
David J. Harvey (poultry, eggs)	(202) 694-5177	djharvey@ers.usda.gov
David J. Harvey (aquaculture)	(202) 694-5177	djharvey@ers.usda.gov
Roger Hoskin (dairy)	(202) 694-5148	rhoskin@ers.usda.gov
Jerry Cessna (dairy)	(202) 694-5171	jgcessna@ers.usda.gov
Sahar Angadjivand (sheep and goats)	(202) 694-5187	sangadjivand@ers.usda.gov
Carolyn Liggon (web publishing)	(202) 694-5056	cvliggon@ers.usda.gov

Subscription Information

Subscribe to ERS e-mail notification service at
http://www.ers.usda.gov/subscribe-to-ers-e-newsletters.aspx to receive timely notification of newsletter availability. Printed copies can be purchased from the USDA Order Desk by calling 1-800-363-2068 (specify the issue number or series SUB-LDPM-4042)

Data Products

Meat Price Spreads, http://www.ers.usda.gov/data-products/meat-price-spreads.aspx, provides monthly average price values, and the differences among those values, at the farm, wholesale, and retail stages of the production and marketing chain for selected cuts of beef, pork, and broilers. In addition, retail prices are provided for beef and pork cuts, turkey, whole chickens, eggs, and dairy products.

Livestock and Meat Trade Data, http://www.ers.usda.gov/data-products/livestock-meat-domestic-data.aspx, contains monthly and annual data for the past 1-2 years for imports and exports of live cattle and hogs, beef and veal, lamb and mutton, pork, broiler meat, turkey meat, and shell eggs. The tables report physical quantities, not dollar values or unit prices. Breakdowns by major trading countries are included.

Related Websites

Livestock, Dairy, and Poultry Outlook,
http://www.ers.usda.gov/publications/ldpm-livestock,-dairy,-and-poultry-outlook.aspx
Animal Production and Marketing Issues,
http://www.ers.usda.gov/topics/animal-products/animal-production-marketing-issues.aspx
Cattle, http://www.ers.usda.gov/topics/animal-products/cattle-beef.aspx
Dairy, http://www.ers.usda.gov/topics/animal-products/dairy.aspx
Hogs, http://www.ers.usda.gov/topics/animal-products/hogs-pork.aspx
Poultry and Eggs, http://www.ers.usda.gov/topics/animal-products/poultry-eggs.aspx
WASDE,
http://usda.mannlib.cornell.edu/MannUsda/viewDocumentInfo.do?documentID=1194

E mail Notification

Readers of ERS outlook reports have two ways they can receive an e-mail notice about release of reports and associated data.

• Receive timely notification (soon after the report is posted on the web) via USDA's Economics, Statistics and Market Information System (which is housed at Cornell University's Mann Library). Go to http://usda.mannlib.cornell.edu/MannUsda/aboutEmailService.do and follow the instructions to receive e-mail notices about ERS, Agricultural Marketing Service, National Agricultural Statistics Service, and World Agricultural Outlook Board products.

• Receive weekly notification (on Friday afternoon) via the ERS website. Go to http://www.ers.usda.gov/subscribe-to-ers-e-newsletters.aspx and follow the instructions to receive notices about ERS outlook reports, Amber Waves magazine, and other reports and data products on specific topics. ERS also offers RSS (really simple syndication) feeds for all ERS products. Go to http://www.ers.usda.gov/rss/ to get started.

U.S. red meat and poultry forecasts

	2011					2012					2013					2014					2015					2016			
	I	II	III	IV	Annual	I	II	III	IV	Annual	I	II	III	IV	Annual	I	II	III	IV	Annual	I	II	III	IV	Annual	I	II	III	Annual
Production, million lb																													
Beef	6,410	6,555	6,736	6,490	26,195	6,282	6,473	6,586	6,572	25,913	6,175	6,513	6,609	6,423	25,720	5,868	6,184	6,179	6,021	24,252	5,664	5,855	6,100	6,175	23,794	5,940	6,545	6,330	24,960
Pork	5,719	5,370	5,484	6,186	22,758	5,858	5,519	5,631	6,244	23,253	5,775	5,516	5,622	6,274	23,187	5,784	5,504	5,424	6,131	22,843	6,161	5,925	5,950	6,545	24,581	6,150	5,945	6,175	24,925
Lamb and mutton	36	40	36	37	149	39	39	39	40	156	38	41	40	38	156	37	43	38	38	156	38	39	37	39	153	38	37	37	151
Broilers	9,290	9,509	9,542	8,861	37,202	9,089	9,381	9,372	9,198	37,039	9,144	9,466	9,683	9,537	37,830	9,283	9,618	9,835	9,814	38,550	9,717	10,020	10,275	10,025	40,037	9,925	10,225	10,475	40,925
Turkeys	1,402	1,471	1,423	1,495	5,791	1,446	1,505	1,480	1,537	5,967	1,459	1,486	1,440	1,420	5,806	1,332	1,428	1,478	1,517	5,756	1,429	1,389	1,325	1,400	5,543	1,350	1,500	1,550	6,010
Total red meat & poultry	23,011	23,114	23,395	23,226	92,746	22,865	23,084	23,274	23,739	92,963	22,743	23,183	23,563	23,844	93,333	22,456	22,934	23,111	23,671	92,171	23,156	23,380	23,836	24,330	94,702	23,546	24,412	24,726	97,589
Table eggs, mil. doz.	1,631	1,644	1,665	1,715	6,652	1,684	1,680	1,707	1,778	6,849	1,733	1,746	1,775	1,825	7,079	1,771	1,799	1,827	1,868	7,265	1,780	1,689	1,625	1,700	6,803	1,700	1,720	1,765	7,015
Per capita disappearance, retail lb 1/																													
Beef	14.1	14.5	14.6	14.0	57.3	14.0	14.6	14.5	14.2	57.3	13.7	14.5	14.3	13.9	56.3	13.1	13.9	13.7	13.4	54.1	13.1	13.6	14.0	13.8	54.5	13.7	14.7	13.7	55.4
Pork	11.4	11.1	11.0	12.2	45.7	11.1	10.9	11.2	12.7	45.9	11.5	11.3	11.4	12.7	46.8	11.3	11.0	11.1	13.0	46.4	12.3	11.8	12.1	13.5	49.7	12.2	11.7	12.4	49.7
Lamb and mutton	0.2	0.2	0.2	0.2	0.8	0.2	0.2	0.2	0.2	0.8	0.3	0.2	0.2	0.2	0.8	0.2	0.2	0.2	0.3	0.9	0.2	0.3	0.2	0.2	1.0	0.3	0.2	0.2	0.9
Broilers	21.5	21.4	20.8	19.1	82.9	20.1	20.4	20.3	19.7	80.4	20.0	20.3	21.0	20.5	81.8	20.2	20.8	21.2	21.1	83.3	21.4	22.1	22.9	22.0	88.3	21.8	22.2	22.7	89.1
Turkeys	3.5	3.5	4.0	5.0	16.1	3.5	3.6	4.1	4.9	16.0	3.7	3.6	4.0	4.9	16.0	3.4	3.5	3.9	5.0	15.7	3.5	3.6	3.8	4.8	15.7	3.3	3.6	4.3	16.2
Total red meat & poultry	51.2	51.2	51.0	51.0	204.5	49.3	50.3	50.6	52.0	202.1	49.5	50.2	51.3	52.4	203.4	48.6	49.8	50.5	53.1	202.0	50.9	51.8	53.2	54.6	210.6	51.7	52.9	53.7	212.8
Eggs, number	61.3	61.5	62.8	64.3	249.9	63.2	62.2	63.3	65.6	254.3	64.3	63.4	64.7	65.6	258.4	64.7	65.3	66.3	66.7	263.0	64.4	61.5	60.1	62.6	248.5	61.6	62.2	63.3	252.6
Market prices																													
Choice steers, 5-area Direct, $/cwt	110.07	112.79	114.05	121.99	114.73	125.29	120.91	119.69	125.54	122.86	125.52	124.95	122.30	130.77	125.89	146.34	147.82	158.49	165.60	154.56	162.43	158.11	144.22	129-135	149-151	131-141	138-150	137-149	136-147
Feeder steers, Ok City, $/cwt	127.20	131.39	134.74	141.93	133.74	152.81	150.05	139.31	143.40	146.39	141.36	133.10	152.08	161.69	147.06	167.49	188.64	220.90	234.25	202.82	210.31	219.69	206.47	187-193	205-208	194-204	201-213	201-213	201-207
Cutter Cows, National L.E., $/cwt	68.66	74.88	66.11	63.54	68.30	76.57	83.51	76.94	73.81	77.71	77.87	76.94	78.36	76.55	77.56	89.12	98.57	111.27	109.50	102.04	107.61	109.50	104.07	98-104	104-106	97-107	102-114	99-111	99-104
Choice slaughter lambs, San Angelo, $/cwt	174.66	157.99	161.13	148.61	160.60	145.33	127.08	89.28	89.85	112.89	107.53	91.72	94.26	111.12	101.16	166.69	148.99	156.02	150.97	155.67	147.17	140.09	144.11	149-155	144-147	145-155	139-151	139-151	142-147
Barrows & gilts, N. base, l.e. $/cwt	59.94	68.80	71.06	64.66	66.11	61.68	61.79	61.43	58.63	60.88	59.03	65.46	70.59	61.11	64.05	68.69	85.40	83.30	66.74	76.03	48.47	53.20	54.59	46-48	50-52	47-51	50-54	50-54	47-50
Broilers, 12 City, cents/lb	80.20	83.00	78.20	78.00	79.90	87.40	85.10	82.00	92.10	86.60	103.50	108.60	93.90	92.80	99.70	98.40	113.70	104.60	102.80	104.90	97.00	104.20	83.70	73-77	89-91	81-87	83-89	87-95	84-90
Turkeys, Eastern, cents/lb	90.20	99.90	106.40	111.60	102.00	100.70	106.90	108.50	106.10	105.60	96.00	97.70	99.90	105.40	99.80	100.70	105.60	110.20	113.90	107.60	99.60	108.50	126.40	131-137	116-118	111-119	112-122	106-114	110-119
Eggs, New York, cents/doz.	105.80	106.60	117.70	131.20	115.30	108.70	99.70	131.90	129.40	117.40	126.90	109.90	119.00	143.00	124.70	142.70	134.60	129.30	162.70	142.30	146.90	170.30	235.70	222-232	193-196	188-202	168-182	149-161	164-178
U.S. trade, million lb																													
Beef & veal exports	633	702	766	683	2,785	558	624	650	620	2,452	557	636	679	717	2,589	583	667	679	644	2,573	526	606	575	575	2,282	520	610	660	2,425
Beef & veal imports	461	593	548	454	2,057	582	669	516	453	2,220	590	629	515	516	2,250	597	767	765	818	2,947	876	991	875	695	3,437	850	850	710	3,045
Lamb and mutton imports	49	48	31	34	162	38	36	38	41	154	49	44	36	44	173	46	49	45	55	195	53	56	43	48	199	50	46	48	190
Pork exports	1,248	1,208	1,260	1,481	5,196	1,442	1,301	1,251	1,386	5,379	1,217	1,225	1,205	1,341	4,988	1,347	1,279	1,090	1,140	4,857	1,165	1,334	1,175	1,325	4,999	1,275	1,300	1,325	5,225
Pork imports	201	195	194	213	803	207	191	198	205	802	208	210	229	233	880	212	240	256	299	1,008	278	264	270	295	1,107	250	225	250	1,000
Broiler exports	1,526	1,598	1,976	1,877	6,978	1,734	1,791	1,864	1,886	7,274	1,752	1,865	1,855	1,874	7,346	1,827	1,834	1,857	1,782	7,301	1,629	1,714	1,575	1,675	6,593	1,675	1,750	1,825	7,100
Turkey exports	159	171	173	199	703	180	184	216	216	797	179	182	198	202	760	163	188	231	223	805	154	123	125	135	537	150	175	200	740
Live swine imports (thousand head)	1,452	1,429	1,407	1,508	5,795	1,445	1,444	1,387	1,380	5,656	1,326	1,285	1,223	1,113	4,948	1,195	1,216	1,264	1,272	4,947	1,312	1,538	1,375	1,300	5,525	1,250	1,250	1,250	5,000

Note: Forecasts are in bold.

1/ Per capita meat and egg disappearance data are calculated using the Resident Population Plus Armed Forces Overseas series from the Census Bureau of the Department of Commerce.

Source: World Agricultural Supply and Demand Estimates and Supporting Materials.

For further information, contact: Mildred M. Haley, (202) 694-5176, mhaley@ers.usda.gov

Updated 10/16/2015

Dairy Forecasts

	2014 IV	2014 Annual	2015 I	2015 II	2015 III	2015 IV	2015 Annual	2016 I	2016 II	2016 III	2016 Annual
Milk cows (thous.) 1/	9,287	9,256	9,305	9,320	9,320	9,325	9,320	9,320	9,315	9,305	9,310
Milk per cow (pounds)	5,487	22,260	5,583	5,757	5,550	5,530	22,420	5,715	5,840	5,665	22,880
Milk production (bil. pounds)	51.0	206.0	51.9	53.7	51.7	51.6	208.9	53.3	54.4	52.7	213.0
Farm use	0.2	1.0	0.2	0.2	0.2	0.2	1.0	0.2	0.2	0.2	1.0
Milk marketings	50.7	205.1	51.7	53.4	51.5	51.3	207.9	53.0	54.2	52.5	212.1
Milkfat (bil. pounds milk equiv.)											
Milk marketings	50.7	205.1	51.7	53.4	51.5	51.3	207.9	53.0	54.2	52.5	212.1
Beginning commercial stocks	12.2	11.2	11.2	13.3	15.6	14.0	11.2	12.2	14.7	15.7	12.2
Imports	1.5	4.3	1.2	1.3	1.6	1.9	6.0	1.3	1.4	1.5	5.9
Total supply	64.5	220.6	64.2	68.0	68.6	67.2	225.1	66.6	70.2	69.6	230.1
Commercial exports	2.3	12.4	2.4	2.5	2.1	2.0	9.0	2.3	2.6	2.6	10.0
Ending commercial stocks	11.2	11.2	13.3	15.6	14.0	12.2	12.2	14.7	15.7	14.0	12.1
Net removals	0.0	0.0	0.0	0.0	0.0	0.0	0.0	0.0	0.0	0.0	0.0
Commercial use	51.0	196.9	48.5	50.0	52.5	53.0	204.0	49.6	52.0	53.0	208.0
Skim solids (bil. pounds milk equiv.)											
Milk marketings	50.7	205.1	51.7	53.4	51.5	51.3	207.9	53.0	54.2	52.5	212.1
Beginning commercial stocks	12.3	11.7	13.1	13.7	14.6	13.9	13.1	13.4	14.0	15.0	13.4
Imports	1.5	5.6	1.4	1.5	1.6	1.9	6.4	1.4	1.6	1.6	6.3
Total supply	64.5	222.4	66.2	68.6	67.7	67.1	227.4	67.9	69.7	69.1	231.8
Commercial exports	9.0	39.1	8.8	10.7	9.5	9.3	38.3	9.2	10.3	10.1	39.5
Ending commercial stocks	13.1	13.1	13.7	14.6	13.9	13.4	13.4	14.0	15.0	14.0	13.5
Net removals	0.0	0.0	0.0	0.0	0.0	0.0	0.0	0.0	0.0	0.0	0.0
Commercial use	42.4	170.2	43.7	43.3	44.3	44.3	175.7	44.6	44.5	45.0	178.8
Milk prices (dol./cwt) 2/											
All milk	22.77	23.97	17.00	16.70	16.75–16.85	17.00–17.40	16.90–17.00	16.00–16.70	15.45–16.45	16.05–17.05	16.05–16.95
Class III	21.19	22.34	15.73	16.24	16.14	15.45–15.85	15.90–16.00	14.35–15.05	14.40–15.40	15.15–16.15	14.75–15.65
Class IV	18.75	22.09	13.62	13.77	13.71	14.45–14.95	13.85–14.05	13.50–14.30	13.60–14.70	14.00–15.10	13.95–14.95
Product prices (dol./pound) 3/											
Cheddar cheese	2.053	2.155	1.567	1.663	1.718	1.705–1.745	1.665–1.675	1.585–1.655	1.560–1.660	1.630–1.730	1.600–1.690
Dry whey	0.625	0.654	0.529	0.444	0.316	0.215–0.235	0.375–0.385	0.235–0.265	0.285–0.315	0.295–0.325	0.280–0.310
Butter	2.140	2.136	1.647	1.838	2.135	2.080–2.150	1.920–1.950	1.850–1.950	1.855–1.985	1.855–1.985	1.840–1.960
Nonfat dry milk	1.379	1.768	1.024	0.948	0.794	0.900–0.940	0.910–0.930	0.900–0.960	0.915–0.985	0.965–1.035	0.960–1.030

1/ Simple averages of monthly prices. May not match reported annual averages.
2/ Simple averages of monthly prices calculated by the Agricultural Marketing Service for use in class price formulas. Based on weekly "National Dairy Products Sales Report".

Sources: USDA National Agricultural Statistics Service, USDA Agricultural Marketing Service, USDA Foreign Agricultural Service, and USDA World Agricultural Outlook Board.
For further information, contact Jerry Cessna, 202-694-5171, jgcessna@ers.usda.gov, or contact Roger Hoskin, 202 694 5148, rhoskin@ers.usda.gov.
Published in Livestock, Dairy, and Poultry Outlook, http://www.ers.usda.gov/publications/ldpm-livestock,-dairy,-and-poultry-outlook.aspx.
Updated 10/16/2015